To Sammy
Love Chr
x

Dog Training Revolution:

2020 Complete Guide to Raising the Perfect Pet with Love

By Russel Embury

Copyright © 2020

ISBN: 9798693992818

CONTENTS

Introduction

For a long time, scientists believed that the friendship between a man and a dog was more than 15,000 years old. But more recently, in the French cave of Chauvet, excavations from the Paleolithic period were carried out. Archaeologists found a wolf's paw print there next to a child's leg. This fact suggests that the domestication of animals began over 30,000 years ago. It means that we have been living "side by side" with our smaller brothers, for a minute, for more than 30 thousand years!

Like humans, dogs have the different temperaments. But often the temperament and behavior of the dog is very often similar to the temperament of its owner. And the longer the dog lives with you, the more it adapts to you and becomes like you. And if you are a cheerful and active person, then the dog resembles you. But, unlike us, our smaller brothers are characterized by some "breed characteristics" that can affect their personality. Therefore, some breeds may be perfect for you, and some may not. I strongly advise you to study the characteristics of the breed of dogs that you want to get for yourself.

It's a big mistake to look for a new friend just by appearance. It's useful to know in advance what type of character the different breeds have, because the dog becomes a real member of the family and a full partner for many years. Therefore, we strongly recommend you to read as much information as possible about the breed of dog that you have chosen. Ask the dog owners in the park or on the social networks about the features, difficulties that they faced to. This is necessary for maximum understanding of what awaits you. Or maybe you are not afraid of difficulties at all and can no longer wait for the moment when such a long-awaited dog will appear at your home.

How to choose a dog

Before getting a dog, it is important to remember that it is a very big responsibility. You should be sure that your lifestyle allows you to adopt a puppy as it will require a lot of your time and attention.

Before you get a dog, there are some questions you need to ask yourself:

Is your lifestyle appropriate for getting a dog?

In order to understand the answer to this question, answer honestly the following questions:

Is the perfect condition of wallpaper and furniture important to you?

How often are you at home and do you have any time for a dog?

Are you allergic to wool?

What do you need a dog for?

Decide for what purpose you want to have a dog. If you are going to walk a lot with the dog in forests and fields, the dog has to be quite hardy. If you want to give a puppy to your grandmother as a present so that she does not feel lonely, do not take a large or hyperactive dog. But for children it is better to have a calm dog of medium or size. This is because small dogs are often treated like dolls by children, and in result the dogs get injured.

Think about it: maybe you are ready to take a dog from a shelter?

Adult dogs with life experience often get to the shelter. It can be grief due to separation from the owner, vagrancy, hunger, fear or distrust of people. Of course, there are quite socialized, contact dogs among shelter dogs, but nevertheless, as a rule, they have already passed the age when it was so important to build the first communication skills with the owner. Much, of course, depends on the conditions in the shelter. Dogs can be kept free, and in an open-air cage for 10-20 animals, and in the individual boxes. The important fact is that who and how communicates with them, how long the dog has been in the shelter. But it is much more difficult to adapt an already formed animal to your lifestyle.

On the other hand, if you take an adult dog, then most likely you will be able to avoid the problems associated with small puppies: puddles on the floor, destruction of shoes, furniture, etc. And, of course, you are given the feeling that you helped this animal and the feeling of gratitude from it.

Chapter 1 Periodization of Dog Development

Scientists have found that development of dogs can be conditionally divided into 5 main stages.

The first stage of development

From the very birth until the 21st day is an adaptation period. During this period, only the innate reflexes play the main role, which determine the survival instincts. Puppies do not see or hear yet, but they can be guided by the smell of their mother, looking for milk. On the 15-18th day of life, their ears and eyes open. A little bit later, they stand on their paws and try to run, so that the initial stage of acquaintance with the outside world begins. By the end of the first stage of development, puppies already react to external stimuli.

The second stage of development

From the 21st to the 35th day is the adaptation period too. This is the period when puppies acquire initial skills. They become more interested in the objects around them and more often move away from their mother.

From the 5th to the 12th week - a period of increased excitability of nerve cells. The stage of "absorption" of information. This period is considered to be the best time for training. Curiosity and research activity at this time allows the owners to develop positive qualities in their pets, which lie in such commands as "Come", "Go outside", "Heel".

The third-fourth stage of development

During the third and fourth stages (from 2 to 7 months), the owner should devote a lot of time to the puppy for walking and training. During this period, puppies begin to acquire their individuality of character, stop reacting "stormy" to the usual external stimuli. Therefore, the owner should organize a search for the correct approach of training - to teach the dog to focus on something, and to be indifferent to something. Now it is a time to teach the further commands like "Stop", "Sit", "Down", "Stand".

The fifth stage of development

The last stage can conditionally last up to 3 years. This time should be devoted to training as much as possible, gradually going through the study and fixing of all the necessary commands.

The most important thing is not to demand a shy little puppy to execute commands that only an adult dog can do. So, gradually, taking into account the physiology and natural instincts of a dog, a person has the opportunity to get a well-mannered friend and helper.

Chapter 2 General information about keeping and custody of a puppy

Every man believes that taking care of a domestic dog is easy. You just need to take them out for a walk and feed them in time. This is a false statement. First you need to understand that caring for an adult dog and caring for a puppy differ. We will first review the caring for a puppy.

Puppy care

Puppies are taken from their mother no earlier than in the age of 1.5 months. In most cases, the age of puppies from 2 to 3 months is the most optimal age to get a puppy.

An exception may be situations when the owner, for some reasons, cannot take such a puppy, or there are small children in the house. In this case, it is better to take the puppy later - at 4–5 months.

Feeding puppies and dogs

This is a very important question, there are two possible options. Either you prepare food for your pets yourself, or you buy ready-made dry or wet food.

It is impossible **to combine** these types of feed, as it can cause indigestion.

The advantage of the ready-made food is that it is developed by specialists taking into account all the nutritional needs of the puppy. The ready-made feed contains an optimal combination of proteins, fats, carbohydrates, vitamins and minerals, there are also omega-3 fatty acids, which ensure the normal development of vision and the nervous system.

But food should not be chosen in economy class, but in super premium class. Only super premium feed contains natural products, they are free of chemicals, dyes and GMOs. It is also allowed to feed the dogs with premium food, but not lower.

Moreover, in a wide range of foods you can find a variety of foods for dogs of different ages, the degree of activity of the pet's lifestyle, and they also take into account the needs for adherence to the diet, if the pet has certain diseases.

The packaging usually lists the diet and serving size for the puppy based on the puppy's weight and age. As a rule, small puppies under one year old are fed 4-6 times a day, then the number of feedings is reduced and by the year it reaches 2-3 times a day.

The best choice of food for your pet is if you consult your veterinarian. Depending on the age of your puppy, its breed, health characteristics and your capabilities, the veterinarian will advise you on the best food in your particular case.

How to get prepared for a puppy in the house?

For puppy care, you will need to arrange a place for

its sleep and feed. You should also buy a dog cage to transport your dog. Take it for growth, taking into account the future size of the maturing puppy. You will need to take the puppy to the veterinary hospital for vaccinations and routine examinations more than once.

Buy bowls for food and water. Wash them thoroughly, change the water in the bowl, it must be fresh. Choose a cozy bed for sleeping. Ask the breeder to bring along a bed with the scent of the puppy's mom, so it will be easier for the puppy to adapt to the new place. Remember, the process of moving to a new place and separation from its mother is a stress for the animal, try to make the process of getting the puppy into your home as comfortable as possible.

Specify what kind of food your puppy has been eating being at the breeder house, ask about the feeding schedule for the portion size. Buy a variety of toys and balls for your puppy, choose products from safe materials, without small parts that the puppy can swallow.

Find out if your puppy is toilet trained. Remember that it will be possible to take the puppy for a walk only after all vaccinations have been made and the puppy was quarantined.

Equip a special place in the apartment where the puppy can relieve itself, put a diaper or newspaper there. A special litter box can be purchased. Teach your puppy to go to a special diaper, wherever it is at this moment, spread the diapers in different places in the house. Then place the diaper on the litter box. This will make it easier for the puppy to understand what actually it has to do. Unfortunately, even if the puppy goes to the toilet in one specific place, this does not mean that it will not make a puddle in another place. Sometimes small puppies can poorly control physiological processes and pee while sleeping. Therefore, these times it is better to remove the carpets in the apartment and cover the furniture with foil.

There are sprays for training your puppy to the litter box. Spray the product on the place you have chosen as a pet toilet (it is usually a special tissue or tray). It is very important that the animal sniffs that area. Use a litter to attract the puppy, spray the lotion on the diaper where it usually "goes to the bathroom" and gradually move the diaper to the area of your choice.

You can also purchase deterrent sprays, which helps to "turn" the puppy against the place where it must not mark a territory.

Scan QR-code:

It will help to stop your puppy from barking at night or when you are away from home.

Visit the veterinarian

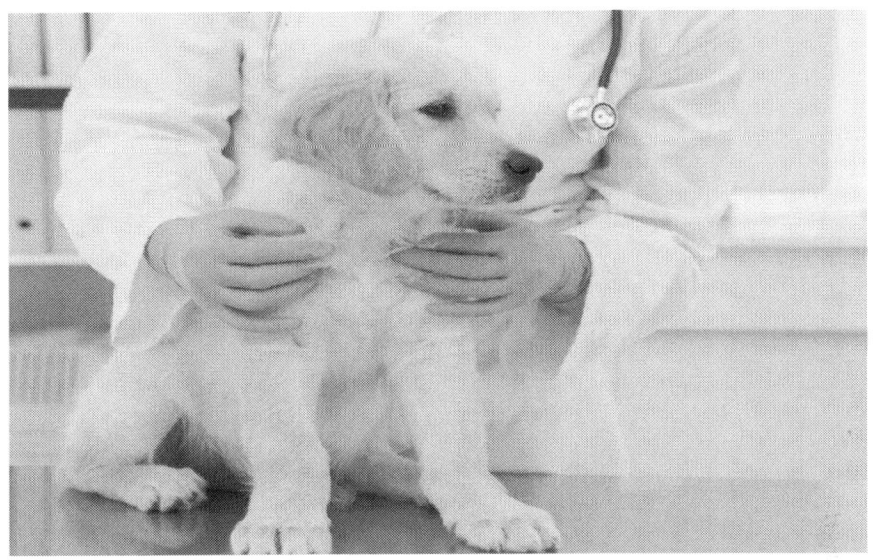

Ideally, it is better to go to the vet with the breeder before you even get the puppy. But if it did not work out, then you should to go to the veterinarian as soon as you get a puppy in order to understand all the nuances about the state of health and get the necessary recommendations.

If you trust the breeder and he has told you about all the nuances about the puppy and told you the time of your next visit for vaccination at the veterinarian - in this case, you don't have to go to the veterinarian again. Then the reason to go to the vet is puppy's bad condition.

But it is very important not to miss vaccinations. Vaccinations play a key role in keeping dogs healthy. Therefore, dogs are taught to visit the veterinarian from a very young age. The veterinarian will tell you in details about when and what vaccination should be done. The first vaccinations should be done at the age of 2 months. Only healthy puppies are vaccinated, beforehand, 15 days before vaccination, it is necessary to conduct anthelminthic therapy for the puppy.

There are two types of vaccinations:

Single vaccines (for one type of disease)

Complex vaccines (against several diseases, for example, plague, rabies, hepatitis, enteritis, etc.)

After vaccination, a very responsible quarantine period begins, which lasts about two weeks. During this period, the puppy's body is weakened and susceptible to diseases, so you need to protect the puppy from all potentially dangerous places of infection with any diseases. The puppy may have a fever, it can feel weakness, and suffers from diarrhea. It is important to discuss with your veterinarian how to behave during this period.

The average cost of a vaccination will be around $ 75-100. This includes core vaccines, which are given in a series of three shots: at 6, 12 and 16 weeks of age.

Major vaccines include DHLPP (plague, hepatitis, leptospirosis, parvovirus, and parainfluenza) vaccines. Your puppy will also need rabies vaccinations, which usually cost around $ 15-20. (Some clinics include this cost in the cost of rabies vaccination.)

Animal shelters often charge less for vaccines - about $ 20 - or vaccines may even be free. If you took your dog from a shelter, he was most likely vaccinated before the age at which you got it. Vaccinations are needed not only for puppies, but every 1-2 years you will have to give your dog a DHPP vaccine.

Ask your veterinarian about the vaccination schedule and don't miss them. Your dog needs to be protected.

Hygiene procedures

It is necessary to bathe your puppy with special puppy shampoos. They take into account that a puppy's coat is softer than an adult dog. Shampoo for an adult dog is not suitable for a puppy. You need to bathe your puppy no more than once a month. Dry your puppy with a dry in silent mode. Train your puppy to comb, especially if your breed has a thick and fluffy coat. You can read about this and much more other information in the next chapter.

Puppy active lifestyle

Games are essential. Puppy care is all about keeping your dog active. Without communication and outdoor games with the owner, the puppy cannot develop harmoniously. Games allow puppy to realize energy, develop muscles, disperse blood, keep the body healthy and strong.

While playing for long hours the puppy is getting ready for adult life, learns to defend his territory and "hunt".

If you have just brought a little puppy to your house and do not know what his temperament is, buy it 5-6 toys of different types to understand which ones it will like the most.

There are these types of toys:

- Ropes (rope for dogs).

Rope toys have three functions. Firstly, they are so-called battering toys. The dog fluttering the rope simulates a fight with the prey, so we recommend to choose a bigger rope so that the dog feels its weight and the "prey" looks realistic. Secondly, due to their elongated shape, the ropes are perfect for teaching the command "Fetch". Third, ropes for dogs are good for the oral cavity. The teeth, penetrating into the cotton fibers, are gently cleaned. Rope toys differ in size.

- Dog balls

Playing with the ball will help the dog to release the

accumulated energy and be in good physical shape. There are several varieties of dog balls: floating balls, squeaky balls or crunchy balls, which are suitable for active play with the dog at home or outside.

- Stuffed Toys

Many dogs are very fond of the plush toys with squeaks: it is pleasant to sleep with them, they are comfortable to carry in their teeth and can be even chewed a little. However, they are not suitable for all breeds of dogs!

- Frisbee

Great toy for older puppies!

- Chewing toys

Chewing toys help the dog relieve stress, clean teeth, massage the gums and they are especially necessary for a puppy during the period of teeth change.

- Pullers

Pullers are toys-shells, the purpose of which is to exhaust your dog, to give it a high-quality physical and mental stress.

Chapter 3 All the wisdom of a domestic dog care

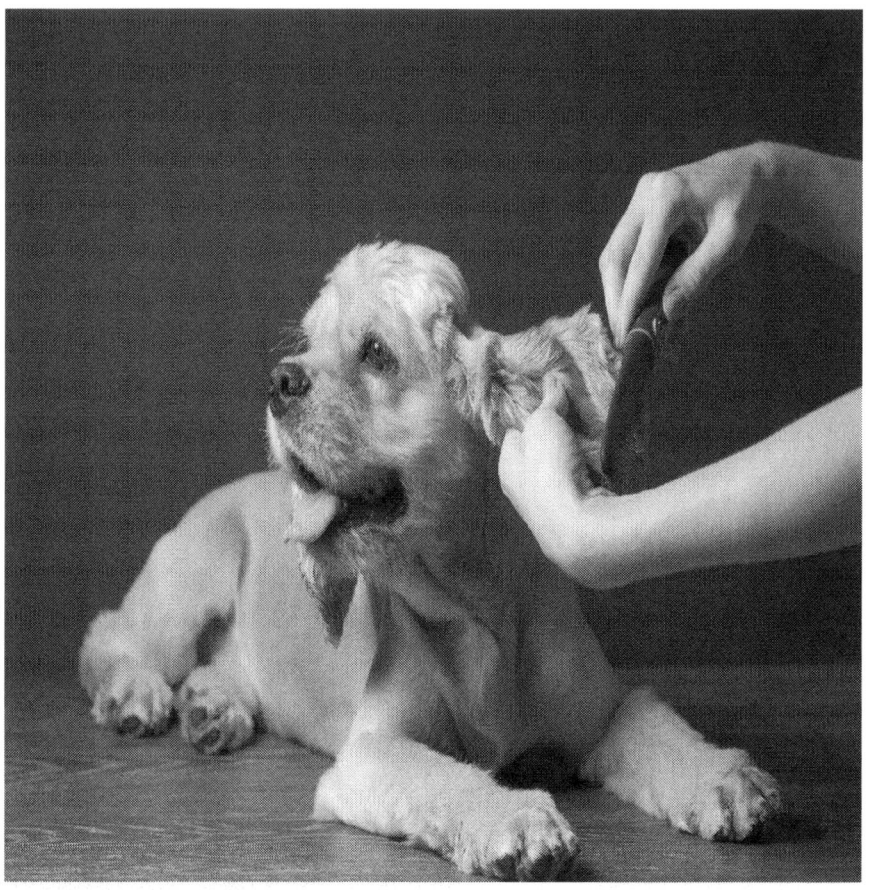

A dog care consists of many factors.
One of the most important aspects of caring for your dog is grooming its coat. It will take a lot of strength

and energy from you, but it is very important.
Caring for your pet's coat directly depends on the
length of this very coat.

**There are four groups of dogs according to
the degree of difficulty in grooming the coat:**

- The first group of dogs is represented by the
  breeds that require the most attention in the
  care of the coat of these breeds. This group
  includes dogs whose hair must be cut and
  plucked. This includes breeds such as terriers,
  cocker spaniels, poodles, schnauzers.
- On the second place in terms of difficulty in
  grooming the coat are breeds of long-haired
  dogs. The coat of these dogs should be
  brushed regularly. This is a truly large group
  of breeds, for example, collie, Pekingese,
  bobtail, etc.
- The next are the short-haired breeds, also a
  really large group, which includes Dobermans,
  Rottweilers, Boxers and many others.
- Dogs that do not have a coat, such as Mexican
  Hairless, Chinese Crested, etc. complete this
  classification. Despite the fact that these dogs
  do not have hair, it does not mean that they do

not need any attention, in contrast, these dogs need special care for their skin.

Daily care of your dog's coat is essential. After all, not only the appearance of the dog depends on this, combing allows you to get rid of dirt, dandruff, dead skin cells, prevents hair from falling off, improves the blood supply to the hairs due to a little massage of the skin with a comb.

So, if you are the owner of a short-haired dog breed, then you will not have any special problems with caring for the dog's coat. For daily care you need a terry towel or a special mitten. Brush your dog twice a week with a hard, natural scrub brush.

If your dog is a long-haired dog, then for grooming you need a comb with long and blunt teeth at the ends. Another tool is a slicker brush, wire brush or, in other words, a slicker.

It is the slicker brush that helps to prevent wool from falling into tangles. However, you cannot use the slicker often, otherwise your dog will become bald. Use the slicker once or twice a month and it will not harm your dog. The slicker and the comb can be used daily only during molting periods. You may also need a special comb - a tangle-cutter, tangles are mainly formed on the legs, behind the ears and in the armpits.

In addition to the slicker, you can purchase a furminator for your pet. The slicker removes the dead wool entrenched in the total wool mass.

Furminator, on the other hand, performs the function of a slicker, but in addition to this, it is able to pull hairs from bulbs that have already died out, but still sitting there.

Furminator is a unique tool and it justifies its cost. And its original is presented EXCLUSIVELY by FURminator (USA). Other manufacturers' tools are fakes. And fakes can harm your pet by ripping pet's back or bald tummy. Consequently, either buy the original or do not buy the furminator at all.

Dogs with very harsh coats need annual haircuts and plucking - trimming. Haircuts are usually done twice a year, according to an individually designed program. The style of haircuts for different breeds may vary slightly each year. If you want to participate in thr exhibitions with your pet, then you need to take into account such fashion trends. Today you can find a wide variety of different types of scissors on the market. However, it is very difficult to make the correct beautiful haircut for a dog on your own and you will hardly be satisfied with the result. It would be better to ask the professionals.

When choosing combs and brushes for your dogs, consult the seller in the pet store, he will help you make the right choice. One general rule for all types of brushes is that the ends of the teeth should be blunt not to damage the dog's skin. The length of the teeth depends on the length of the dog's coat, the longer the coat, the longer the teeth of the brush. The density of the teeth also depends on the density of the coat. The owner of the dog should have two types of brushes with sparse teeth for quick combing and more frequent teeth for more careful brushing.

For daily grooming of dogs with harsh hair, use combs with hard metal teeth. Schnauzers and terriers are necessary to be wiped the beard after feeding with a mitten and periodically combed it with a brush.

Bathing dogs

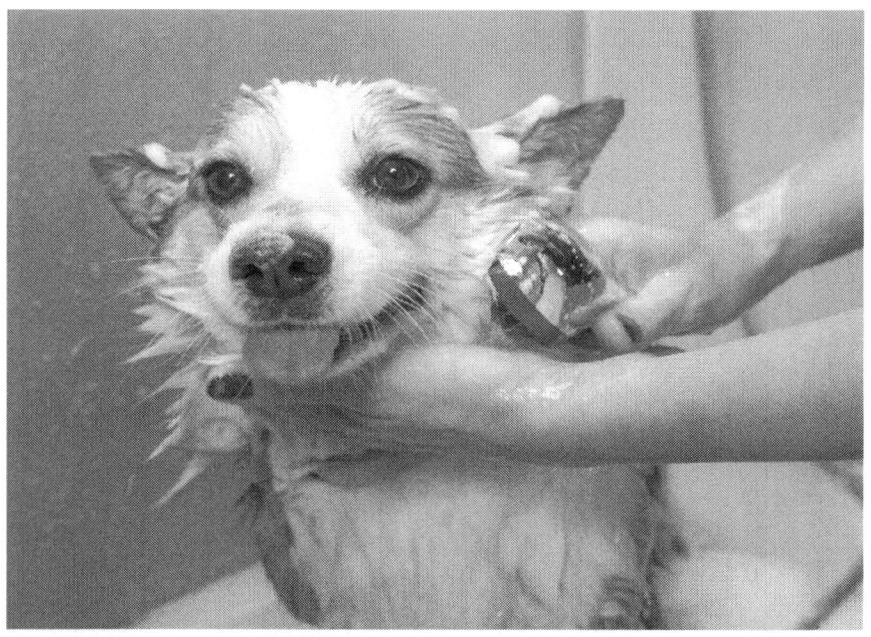

Dog grooming includes bathing. Bathing frequency also depends on the dog's coat type.

For long-haired dogs with a coat tend to tangles, more frequent bathing and careful brushing are desirable. For short-haired dogs, bathing is less frequent, about once a month. Bathing water should fit the dog's body temperature and vary between 37.5-39 ° C.

You need to dry long-haired dogs with a hairdryer, wipe short-haired dogs thoroughly with a terry towel.

There is a wide variety of special shampoos and conditioners, which suit coat types and coat care needs.

The main criteria for choosing a shampoo

When buying a shampoo for a person, we pay attention to the brand, condition and length of our hair, the desired result. Here is the same situations for dogs.

When choosing a shampoo for a dog, one should consider:

1) Dog breed and coat type
These two factors are the main when choosing a

shampoo. For dogs with soft coats, such as the Poodle breed, you should buy a soft coat shampoo to avoid churning. Harsh-coated breeds such as terriers need to be softened the coat and increased the shine. Long-haired dogs need to be made combing easier and make their hair more elastic. Therefore, when choosing a cosmetic product, you need to consult a veterinarian or seller not to harm your dog.

2) Skin condition and coat type

If the dog's skin becomes oily or, on the contrary, dry, an allergic reaction or dandruff appears, then these factors must also be taken into account. After all, the aim of the composition of each shampoo is to solve a specific problem or prevent it.

3) The presence of parasites (if your pet has fleas, or it had a mite recently removed, then in these cases there are shampoos that will suit your dog better). But if fleas or mites appear, you have to contact your veterinarian!

The best dog shampoos should be free of chemicals and fragrances. If possible, it is better to give preference to products from well-known manufacturers (often popular brands include only natural ingredients), or ask your groomer for advice on choosing a shampoo.

You also need to consider that dogs also have allergies. If your dog suffers from it, in this case, you should not independently experiment choosing the hypoallergenic remedy or shampoo. You would better go to the vet, find out the reason of this reaction and choose the right care product with him.

In general, the composition of the shampoo may contain:

- Healing herbs (usually they are needed to eliminate dandruff and dryness, have a moisturizing effect);
- Oat extract (also moisturizes and is suitable for dry wool);
- Aloe vera extract (suitable for sensitive skin with irritation or itching, allergy sufferers);
- Tea tree extract or tea tree oil (have an antiseptic effect);
- Panthenol (softens, adds shine);
- Coal tar - the component that will help to get rid of dandruff with increased sebum secretion (usually with eczema or seborrhea, the veterinarian will tell you about this);
- Proteins and panthenol- components that add silkiness and shine to the coat,

Dry shampoo can be used for dogs that, according to indications, are prohibited from swimming (after surgery, etc.). This powder is applied to the coat, left on for a while to absorb excess oil, and then simply combed out with a brush.

Attention! This type of shampoo cannot be used on a permanent basis, only temporarily and only if there is no other way out. It is best to consult a veterinarian before use.

Clipping your dog's nails

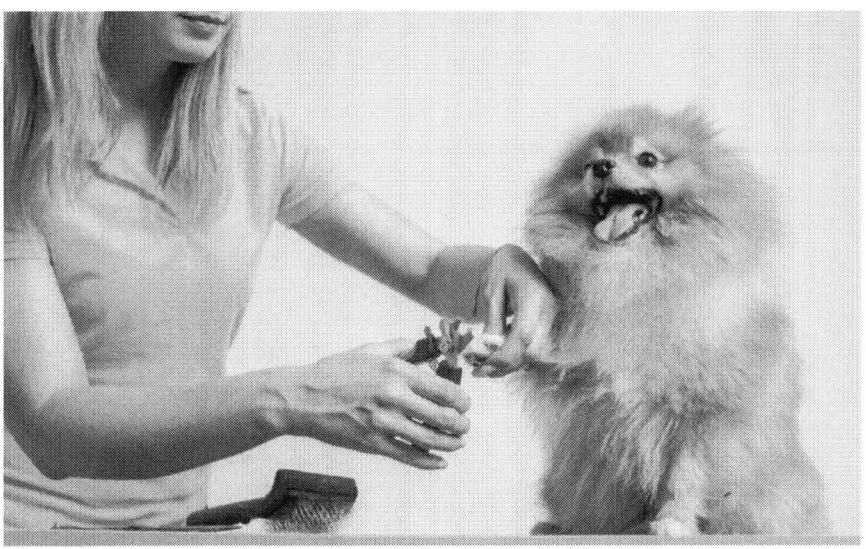

Besides the coat, it is also necessary to trim the claws of the dog. Approximately every 7-10 days, and it is important not to touch the blood vessel in the cavity of the claw, which is located at the base. Excess hair is also cut on the paws, while the style of the haircut corresponds to the breed of the dog. Tangles are often formed on the paws, they need to be combed out and cut. You should also check the paws daily for dirt, glass and other contaminants.

In winter, the streets and roads are sprinkled with reagents, so after a walk you need to wash your pet's paws with water and soap. In the summer, it is enough to wipe the dog's paws after a walk with a clean cloth. If the skin on the paw pads is cracking, then lubricate them with a greasy cream.

A dog nail clipper is a necessary tool, since the claws, growing back, cause inconvenience to the animal. Excessively long claws spread apart the paw pads, which can lead to muscle atrophy.

Doing the first clipping of the claws, it is better to contact a groomer at the age of 3 months, not earlier, since up to 3 months the claws are very fragile and brittle, not fully strengthened.

What is the tool for?

On the lateral and dewclaws, the claws of dogs do not reach the ground, so they do not grind due to the long walks on the street. They should be given special attention: if you do not cut them in time, the claws grow into the skin.

In order not to injure your pet, do not use ordinary household scissors to care for paws in any case! For these purposes, you need to choose a special device.

Types of nail clippers

At the pet store, you can find two varieties of this tool:

The sickle-shaped nail clipper looks like tweezers with two curved blades. The width of their opening is regulated with the help of a limiter. It can be adjusted to fit the size and thickness of the claw. This nail clipper is suitable for large dogs with strong nails.

The guillotine claw is shaped like a ring into which a pet's claw is inserted for a haircut, with two blades. It is designed for medium and small breeds.

When choosing, pay attention on the size of the pet's claw and your own hand, so that you can comfortably hold the claw.

How to train your dog to clip its nails

The process of getting used to the clipping is quite time-consuming and it runs gradually. If you follow a few simple rules, it will go as easy as possible for you and your four-legged friend.

You need to accustom the dog to the clipping from a young age. Let it "get acquainted" with the device, gently move them along the claws.

Hold the pet's paw in your hand before the procedure. Be sure to praise your dog if it sits calmly. If the animal breaks out, gets nervous, it is better to pause the learning process and repeat later.

When the dog learns to respond to the nail clipper calmly, you can start cutting. Do not process all the claws at once. Do this gradually. Do not force your pet, it should get used to this process in a calm environment.

How to use it correctly

Prepare a blood stopping agent (styptic stick or talcum powder) and an antiseptic before starting the procedure. The clipping should be done in a good lighting.

Fix the dog's paw and gently press down on the pad to reveal the claw. Examine it carefully.

You should see a blood vessel - the edge of the stratum corneum that you don't need to go beyond. Cut the claw at a right angle perpendicular to its surface. Do not hurry. Sometimes the blood vessel is very poorly visible and then it is better not to cut, than cut off more than needed and hurt your dog.

At the end of the procedure, trim the cut claws with a nailfile.

The first clipping can be done by a veterinarian or groomer in your presence. Having observed his actions, you will learn how to handle your pet's claws by yourself.

What to do with injuries

The dog often bleeds heavily, if it is injured while clipping.

If you do not have a special styptic pencil at hand (you can buy it in any veterinary pharmacy and keep it at hand for such cases), then you can use talcum powder. But for the future you will definitely need such a pencil.

It is very important to remember that all solutions that contain alcohol will only increase the pain if there is a wound and it cannot be used.

Teeth and gum care

For puppies for complete care, it is enough to wipe the teeth and gums with special napkins for the oral cavity.

The teeth and gums of adult dogs are mechanically cleaned from plaque, preventing the formation of tartar. If it was not possible to prevent the formation of tartar, you would need to contact your veterinarian. To avoid calculus formation, you need to brush your dog's teeth with a special tooth powder or toothpaste and brush for dogs. At the end, you should wipe the polished teeth with a soft cloth.

It is very important to brush your dog's teeth regularly. Small breed dogs are more prone to dental problems.

Never use human teeth care products, use only dog-specific products.

The most common types of brushes:

Brushes with bristles or rubber teeth and a handle;

Finger brushes or fingertips.

It is worth remembering that you need to use the bristled brushes carefully, as too intense brushing can injure the gums.

Brushing a dog's teeth isn't much different from how humans do it. However, for the animal (and therefore for the owner), this process is far from the most pleasant. Therefore, it is important to teach your pet to this procedure as early as possible: at puppyhood, dogs quickly adapt to everything new, so it is better to teach your dog to brush his teeth in 2-3 months.

1. The pet must be fixed. For a large dog it would be easier to brush its teeth when it is sitting. Small breed dogs can be placed on the table;

2. Brushing pet's teeth is stressful, so be sure to calm your pet. It will be most convenient if someone from the family helps you with this. This way you will not be distracted by the encouragement of your pet, and the cleaning will be faster;

3. You should start brushing from the farthest teeth. This is due to the fact that pulling the lip will cause fewer negative emotions for the dog than lifting the nose;
4. You should start brushing the teeth from the outside and closer to the gums, this is where tartar forms;
5. After the dog gets used to brushing the outside of the teeth, you can gradually move on to brushing the inside part;
6. Do not try to brush all the teeth at once. You should train your pet gradually, each time covering more and more teeth. If your dog does not let you open its mouth, don't force it. It will only turn the dog against the procedure.
7. When brushing is finished, do not forget to reward your pet.

The special chewy treats can also be used to prevent plug and tartar.

But don't forget that these treats contain extra calories.

Ear cleaning

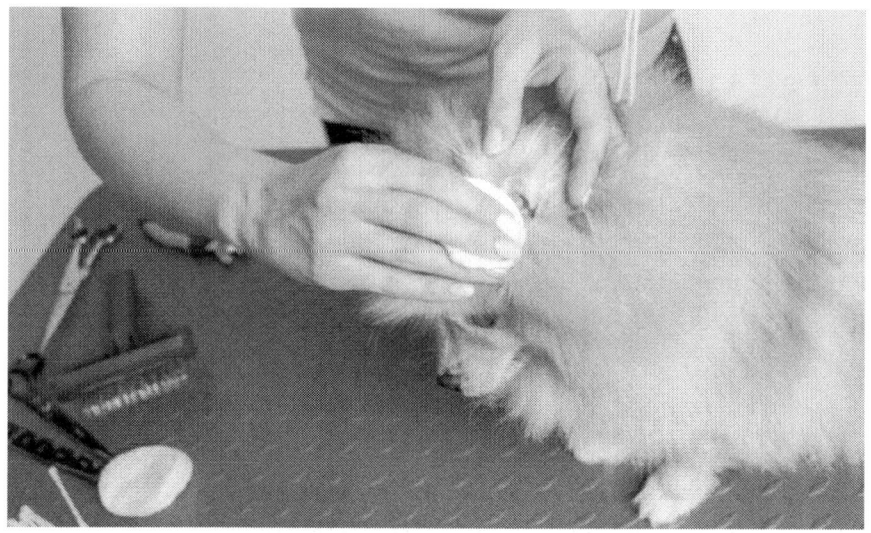

One of the most important hygiene procedures is cleaning your pet's ears. You need to check and clean your pet's ears regularly.

Timely hygiene procedure can prevent the development of inflammation of the auricle – otitis and eliminate the infiltrated parasites.

When cleaning the ears, it is important to remember not to overdo it, otherwise you could injure your dog.

In this case, you need to know that earwax and sebum play an important role in the body. They are a barrier against external factors, protecting the ear canals from the dust particles and mites contained in it, temperature changes, etc. Therefore, such formations in the ears must be present in small quantities, otherwise the organ will be defenseless against pathogenic microorganisms.

You need to clean your dog's ears without using physical force, do not rub sensitive skin, achieving perfect cleanliness. Otherwise, microscopic cracks appear on the skin, which subsequently become inflamed and can become infected with various fungus or bacteria.

Before cleaning, you need to make sure that the procedure is necessary. There can be some difficulties with dogs with sagging ears and long-haired pets while cleaning. Standing auricles have good ventilation, so they stay clean for a longer time, as dirt does not stick to them and the sebaceous glands do not become cluttered.

A frequency of this procedure depends on many factors. You should rarely clean the ears of a young and healthy animal. Dogs living in apartment conditions also do not need frequent cleaning.

Some dogs with standing, open ears may not need to be cleaned at all, but in any case, you need to examine them carefully, at least once every 7-10 days and after each walk to check that your pet has not picked up any mites.

You can do a test: slightly moisten a cotton swab and wipe the ear near the ear canal, but without penetration. If you find a small coating of gray or yellow on the stick, do not worry - the ears do not require a cleansing procedure. But if there are sulfur lumps on the cotton wool, then it's time to clean the pet's ears.

Special ear cleaners

Nowadays there are many different products on sale for this purpose. You can choose any, based on your own preferences:

- Special wet wipes – they are good because the substances impregnating them dissolve well dirt deposits, but at the same time are suitable for sensitive dog skin.
- Cotton swabs for cleaning animal ears - they differ from ordinary sticks in that they are impregnated with special solutions.
- Lotions for ear hygiene - have high absorbent characteristics, not only collecting impurities, but also removing them from the ears by means of massage, or while shaking off the pet.
- Cleaning powder - great for dogs with long ears. They eliminate excess moisture, improve ventilation of the auricle, and protect against dirt accumulation and contamination. All this prevents the development of fungal diseases.

One should conduct the procedure being prepared - having at hand cotton swabs, gauze, cotton wool, warm boiled water.

An appropriate time to clean the ears is when the animal is calm and relaxed. It is necessary to sit down with the pet, caress it, massage the ears, and in such a situation the dog will feel comfortable. At this moment, you cannot raise your voice to the dog, use brute force.

You can use another technique based on the pleasant associations of the animal related to walking. While putting on a collar and leash, the pet knows that this is a mandatory procedure, so it does not get nervous. This manipulation has a disciplinary effect and will allow cleaning without any problems. In most cases, dogs quickly get used to cleaning their ears.

Encouragement is another powerful method that can be used while cleaning the ears. Then the pet will patiently endure everything if it is sure to receive some treats at the end.

You should not put any pressure on the dog, trying to fix it in one position. Such actions lead to the fact that the animal is frightened or shows aggression. The pet can be held by clasping the head with your hands, or by lightly tugging on the collar.

If we are talking about cleaning the ears at home, then you should not trust this business to people unfamiliar to your pet. A dog that does not trust a person will not allow him to carry out such a manipulation.

After the procedure, in addition to a rewarding treat, it is necessary to praise the dog, caress it so that the pet understands that its behavior is a reason for praise.

If there is no desire or opportunity to clean the ears by yourself, then you can ask the professionals for help by visiting a veterinary clinic.

If, during the manipulations, inflammation, bad-smelling discharge, black dots on the surface were found, then most likely we are talking about infection or parasite infestation. In this case, you must immediately visit the clinic, or call a veterinarian at home.

Chapter 4 Dog Training

The very word training comes from the French "dresser" and means to teach. It means that the dog is taught to perform certain actions according to certain commands by voice or conventional gestures.

It is necessary to separate the concepts of training and education immediately. It is important not to mix these both.

Education begins from the first minutes when the puppy appears in your house. For good breeders, education begins from the moment the puppy opens its eyes and begins to explore the territory. A well-bred dog may be left without training. But it is impossible to train an ill-bred dog.

A good relationship with a person is the key to a good dog upbringing. It is the quality of these relationships that is very important, the quantity to a lesser extent. You can sit at home for half a day with the dog and ignore it. But you also can play for an hour, repeat a few commands and go for a short walk.

Nowadays there are many different types and systems of dog training in the world. All of them can be conditionally divided into two large groups. The first group - the smaller one - is obedience. This is the base that is found in all types of training. It is due to the fact that communication with a dog that does not know elementary commands is very difficult or not possible at all, not to mention the further training.

The general training includes the commands necessary in daily communication with the dog for trouble-free communication and are also useful for both humans and dogs. These are the commands "Come!", "Stop!", "Heel!", "Place!", "Sit!", "Down!" etc.

The second part is special training. Here, training is mainly carried out on a professional basis, so you can turn to a dog handler and he will show you how to train a dog properly. Ideally, you can also contact a dog handler for training on basic commands.

It is obligatory to raise and train a dog in obedience. It is up to you to decide to what extent and in what way to train your dog. As for special types of training, whether to train them or not depends only on your desire and capabilities.

Accustoming to a nickname, leash, etc.

- Accustoming a puppy to a nickname

The name of a dog is the first and also the most frequently used command. As a result of accustoming to a nickname, a dog develops a persistent skill — to pay attention immediately to its owner after he calls its nickname. Thus, the nickname acquires the conventional meaning of the signal "attention" for the dog.

Usually, dogs are accustomed to the nickname at the age of puppyhood (from the first month). Sometimes it is necessary to accustom an adult dog to a nickname: when the dog passes to a new owner (when its nickname is unknown), when the nickname changes.

First and foremost, the nickname should not be long and difficult to pronounce. It is better if it is a short and sonorous word that is easy to remember.

As soon as the puppy crosses the threshold of the new home, call it only by the chosen name. The puppy needs to get used to a particular word and learn the connection between it and the action. That is why it is very important at first not to use diminutive nicknames, new names and not to call the puppy with a whistle or with the help of other sounds. All this will disorient the animal: the puppy will pay attention to any similar sounds, react to calls from strangers.

Memorizing a nickname is the foundation of training. A nickname for a dog is an association of close contact with the owner. It is possible and necessary to speed up the process of memorizing a name with positive backup - verbal praise, caress or a piece of food. When pronouncing a nickname, watch the puppy's reaction: as soon as it reacts and turns to you, give it a piece of food and praise immediately.

Repeat the name of the puppy before each feed, placing a bowl of food in front of it only after the puppy had reacted to its name and come up to you.

- Leash and collar training

Leash and collar are essential accessories for every domestic dog. Any walk, visit to the doctor, or even

just going out to a public place should be accompanied by these two items. This is necessary for the safety of people around and the dog itself. The collar is much easier. Even from the birth, babies can wear a thick thread around their necks, then change it to a light collar. Things stand more complicated with a leash.

How to choose a leash?

First of all, the leash should be comfortable and soft and picked up individually. It should not pinch anything or rub anything. Natural materials and maximum delicacy are the basic requirements for a puppy leash. Also, the first leash should be short, be as lightweight and simple as possible. Make sure that the leash does not have any strong smell. If the smell is present, then after purchase, let it lie at home for a few more days until the smell disappears.

First steps:

The ideal age for leash training is the first one and a half to two months. Earlier this period, puppies are not yet very conscious. Later, they acquire their own character, which can make the process difficult.

The first fitting should last no longer than a few minutes. Distract the puppy with something interesting at this time, do not let it play with the string itself.

All the first steps should take place at home in a familiar territory for the puppy, and after the first positive results, you can try to put on the leash on the street.

Also, being at home, rehearse walking in the direction set by the owner. At first it will be extremely difficult, but over time the puppy will begin to obey. Then change your collar to a light collar or bark collar by perforce scan QR-code to learn more:

Features of collar and leash training for adult dogs

This need arises much less frequently, but it is a more difficult task. An adult dog has an established character and it is not so easy to inculcate new habits in it, but it is quite possible. The situation with collar is not critical, but the leash requires more attention and patience.

The main thing is to make it clear to the dog that the

leash does not pose a threat. Make sure that the leash is long enough to allow the dog to get far from you. This will allow it not to feel a strong restriction of freedom.

You should walk only in familiar areas at first. It is not necessary to hold the leash constantly in your hands. Let it reach for the dog, and you can only occasionally lift the leash, but in way not to frighten the dog.

To make the dog associate the leash with pleasure, show it every time you are going to go outside with it. To teach the dog to stop when needed - just stop yourself, and pull on the leash and at the dog's incomprehensible glance, call it to you and give something tasty. To begin with, it will be enough to walk at least thirty meters. Over time, the duration of these walks can be increased. Get ready that it will take a month or more for an adult dog to develop all the necessary reflexes.

It is also worth making sure that the dog is able to walk next to the owner, because walks together are not always limited to just walking in the park.

You can consult a veterinarian and / or dog handler in more detail on how to teach an adult dog to a collar and leash, paying attention to age, breed and character traits. After all, most cases are individual.

Training to clean and wash

The animal should take a shower every time an unpleasant smell comes from its fur. It is not advisable to bathe adult dogs as well as puppies more than once every 2 weeks. Without external contamination, the dog's coat turns oily 6-7 weeks after the last bath.

In general, the frequency of washing depends on several factors, including breed, activity, and participation in exhibitions. After daily walks, it is enough to wash the dog's paws and stomach with clean warm water, comb out the coat too, freeing it of stuck lumps of dirt.

To train your dog to water painlessly, follow these tips:

- Let the puppy "get to know" the water better. Use basins or other containers filled with water. Take a rubber toy and throw it on the surface, luring the pet this way. Never force the baby, as in the future it will cause even greater "dislike" for the wet environment;
- To train your dog to bathe gradually, wash its paws regularly. Even if they are not dirty, it will help the dog to get used to the water faster. The majority of animals are calm about washing their paws, and they even have a reflex - they themselves give their paw to their owner;
- How to bathe your dog in the bathroom? Very often our pets want to jump out and run away. Use a treat and your caress to train your pet. Start by luring the dog into an empty bathroom and letting it sit there for a while. Repeat the command "wash", "swim" "in the

bath" so that the baby perceives, and for the implementation - indulge it in goodies;

- Put the tap on and let the water flow out in a thin stream. The temperature should be medium. The lathering procedure is perceived more calmly if the dog is already used to bathing. The main thing is to make sure that the care products do not get into his ears and eyes.

It is also necessary to teach your pet to swim in reservoirs, a pool. Choose the shallow and warm lakes or reservoirs with a gentle bank for this. It is advisable to carry small dogs on hands, after - gradually take your hands off, giving the dog the ability to swim on his own. If your pet barks or whines with fear, do not force it, because the feelings of the smaller brothers also need to be respected.

Accustoming to sound and light stimuli

Dogs, even in puppyhood (4-5 months), during socialization must be taught to various stimuli. For example, to sound: thunder, fireworks shots. Light: lights from car headlights, floodlights, etc. Before proceeding to basic obedience training, special training a dog must be taught to be indifferent to distractions.

It is best to train your dog to various sound and light stimuli during walks, carefully observing the behavior of the dog. At the same time, the power of the stimulus should not frighten and oppress the dog.

Acoustic stimulation training (you need an assistant):

- While the dog is eating, your helper, being in another room, sharply strikes with an iron object on a can (basin), or other iron object;
- If the dog starts to worry, you should ignore the sound so that the dog understands that there is nothing wrong;

Repeat this practice several times a day until the dog stops worrying and shows only alertness.

While walking with the dog, ask your assistant at a distance of 50 meters to fire a firecracker (launch fireworks), if possible, shoot with sport gun or starter pistol. Watch your dog at this time: if it starts to worry, keeping its tail tucked fearfully - switch its attention to something else, distract the dog. If the dog reacts calmly to the shots, ask your friend to come closer to you with the dog and make shots at a distance of 20 m. And so on - gradually, when the dog gets used to the shots, reduce the distance between you and your helper to 10 meters and repeat the exercise again. Do not also forget to be safe, and conduct training in deserted places not to harm others.

If the dog is very anxious, then it is best to switch its attention to playing with the ball, running with it, wrestling, etc.

If there is an opportunity, it is good to be with the dog next to the railway, so that it gets used to it and does not react to the noise of the train passing by.

The skill is considered to be developed when the dog at any time of the day and under any circumstances will fearlessly treat noises, claps, shots.

How to stop chewing

Most puppies start chewing on things when their teeth are teething. As they grow up, they begin to chew on toys during play, or other things out of boredom or following instinct. Your dog may start chewing on things in unfamiliar surroundings due to separation anxiety. Identifying the cause of this behavior is key to prevent it.

If your dog chews on everything in the house, regardless of whether you are nearby or not, it may be due to boredom. It probably needs more play, exercise and activity in order to expend excess energy. Buy special toys to help keep your dog from chewing on things.

Do not hurry to punish the puppy for what it is not guilty. It wants to chew - let it chew, but not just anything, but special treats for dogs and toys, which should be enough to distract the puppy's attention from your things.

As soon as you notice that the dog is chewing on everything that catches its eye, take measures. Remove from the puppy's field of vision those objects that may be of interest to its curious nature - shoes, books, wires, household appliances, trash can, small objects that can be swallowed. The less temptation - the better.

Teach your puppy to chew only on specially designed items. Changing teeth of puppies may be accompanied by itching. You should never let your puppy scratch its teeth on your old clothes or shoes, even if you were about to throw them away! A "taboo" on other people's things should be developed in the baby's mind. It is necessary to teach the puppy to chew only on permitted objects, and this rule also applies to adult dogs. You have to teach your dog how to entertain itself correctly and achieve unmistakable behavior without leaving it unattended.

It often happens that the dog chews on things even though the owner is present. An untrained animal does not know your rules yet, so it is useless to be angry at his misdeeds, especially to punish. It's better to teach your dog to behave correctly and watch it. If there are no such possibilities, then leaving the house, leave the dog where it will not harm property. It is only important to leave many interesting permitted toys for the dog that will entertain it until you come back.

The only way to stop your dog from chewing on things is to catch it "in the act." If you find a shoe that was damaged by a dog within an hour after it "worked" on it, the dog will not be able to correlate the received punishment with what it did. The dog may look "guilty" when you show it a spoiled thing, but this is just a manifestation of subordinate behavior. But if you find the dog at the moment when it is chewing on something, be sure to stop it with some command or with a loud voice. If it obeys you and leaves the thing alone, give it a special toy. If the dog starts chewing on a toy, be sure to praise it.

There are special sprays that can be applied to various things to prevent the dog from chewing them on. Such foods have a taste or smell that is unpleasant to the dog but imperceptible to humans.

And, as always, you should consult your veterinarian and / or dog handler. They will be able to give you valuable advice on how to correct such behavior.

Come

The command "Come" is considered to be one of the most important, and every dog should be trained to teach it - both shepherd, Labrador, and York. Teaching the command "Come" does not require strong emotional or physical pressure on the dog, so puppies can be taught this command from the age of 1.5 months.

In everyday life, it is enough for the dog to just walk up to you and sit down. It is important that when the dog comes to you, it has not to just stand and look around, but sit down, because in this way it is distracted from his affairs and concentrates its attention on you.

So, how do you teach a dog the "Come" command?

It is best to start training at home or in a quiet

outdoor location so that no background noise will distract your pet.

To do this, you will need a treat and a treat bag.

Remember, calling your dog should be done in a funny manner. Never punish your dog if it comes up to you on its own. Otherwise, the puppy will perceive the call as a threat and will refuse to approach you, on command or without it. Prepare a treat in a pocket or special bag. Standing in a free position, cheerfully, loudly and clearly shout out the name of the dog and then give the command "Come". When the puppy pays attention to you and starts moving into your direction, praise it in a jolly voice. If the puppy does not respond to the command, make any loud sound to get its attention. As soon as it looks at you, start moving away from the puppy and repeat the command. As soon as it is near you, give it a treat and caress it actively. Then let it go for a walk again. Repeat the steps above several times.

After the skill has been worked out, we complicate the task, we teach the puppy to come on the first try. You will need a treat and a treat bag to do this.

When the puppy learns to approach you systematically on command, let us proceed to the next step. Prepare a treat in a pocket or special bag. Shout out the dog's name in a fun manner, then give the command "Come" and slap your hand on your leg. Wait silently for the dog to come up to you. As soon as the dog comes up to you, praise it with a treat and caress it actively. If the puppy pauses halfway to you or decides to change the "route", shout out its nickname and again slap on your leg. Do not repeat the command "Come" a second time.

After that we will complicate the "Come" command by adding a background stimulus.

You will need a treat, a treat bag and 2-3 toys to do this.

When the puppy learns to follow the command "Come" without repetition, complicate it with stimuli, which can be people or toys. Prepare a treat, cheerfully shout out the nickname and give the command "Come", while the dog runs towards you, throw the toy aside. When the dog is near you, praise it with a treat and actively pet it. If the dog is distracted, shout out the nickname and additionally give the command "Come" along with a slap on the leg. You can use a sound that attracts the puppy. When the dog is near you, praise it with a treat and actively pet it. Dogs learn the exercise very quickly, so after 1-2 days you can increase the distance and bring it up to 5 meters (use a long leash for this). Also, start petting the approaching dog before giving it a treat - this way you will teach it to be given in your hands (the dog will understand - if the name is called, it is for a reason). Continue practicing the "Come" command while walking and call the dog every 10-15 minutes to hone the skill. Be sure to pet and reward your pet when it comes up. At first, it is not recommended to call your dog if it is busy with something, as it hardly listens to you. Work with the dog every day and over time complicate the exercise - enter the command "Sit" (we will describe how to teach the dog to this command below), and also increase the distance and change the environment so that the dog learns to approach on command in any situation.

Sit

The command to sit in dog training is one of the basic exercises. This command is very important for training attention to a person and developing discipline during endurance training.

This skill is included in all disciplinary training courses and in almost all disciplines of dog sports;

Dog sitting helps to fix it in a calm position and, if necessary, leave it in this position for a certain time;

In fact, having taught the dog the command "Sit", you gain control over it and at any time you can use the position to care for the ears, eyes, hair of the dog, moreover you can give it a calm state when putting on the collar and muzzle, restraining its attempts to jump on you or run out the door earlier than needed etc.

Having taught the dog to sit, you can successfully work out with it the skills of showing attention, the game "Paw" and many other tricks.

You will need a treat.

Prepare a treat in your hand or a special bag. Call the dog over to you. As soon as it comes up to you, let it smell the delicacy, give the command "Sit" by voice and gesture. Place the gesture with treat slightly behind the dog's head. Pause. When the dog sits down, praise it with a voice and give it a treat. Then caress it over its chest. Let the dog walk for 1-2 minutes, then repeat the exercise again. If the dog is trying to reach for the treat, or jumping, bring the treat behind the dog's head again and apply a little pressure on the croup. Pause 3-5 seconds. During the pause, the dog must sit. Then knock the dog down with your voice and treat. Caress it over its chest.

After developing the skill, we complicate the task: Calling + Sitting

Now we will analyze two options for dog sitting, namely in front of the owner and near the leg.

To do this, you will need a treat.

We teach the dog to sit in front of the owner. Prepare a treat in your hand or a special bag. From a free position, call the dog, when it is in front of you, let it smell the treat out and bring it a little behind the dog's head. There is no need to say the "Sit" command. When the dog sits down, give it a treat and compliment it with your voice. If the dog does not sit down, give some light pressure to the croup. Pause for 3-5 seconds and praise your dog with a treat. The second option for sitting is sitting near your leg. Prepare a treat in your hand or in a special bag. From a free position, call the dog when he is in front of you, let it smell the treat out and circle your hand with the treat around you, sitting the dog on the right side. Let me remind you that to sit the dog, you need to bring the treat a little behind the dog's head. When the dog has sat down, pause for 3-5 seconds and praise the dog with your voice and treats. Pet the dog.

Please note:

- While practicing the skill of sitting, give the command once, do not repeat it several times;
- Make the dog perform the technique after the first command;
- When practicing a technique, the command given by voice is always primary, and the actions you perform are secondary;
- If, nevertheless, it is necessary to repeat the command, you should act more decisively and use a stronger intonation;
- Over time, gradually it is necessary to complicate the technique, starting its development in a comfortable environment for the dog;
- Regardless of the chosen method of practicing the technique, do not forget to encourage the dog with a treat and petting after each of its implementation, telling it "Good, sit";
- It is very important not to distort the command. It should be short, clear and always sound the same. Therefore, instead of the command "Sit", you cannot say "Sit down", "Come on, sit", etc.;

- A method of "sitting" can be considered learned by the dog, when it sits down at your very first command and remains in this position for a certain amount of time;

Down

You can start practicing laying skills with a puppy at the age of 2.5-3 months, but firstly you need to teach the puppy to sit down on command. From a sitting position, it is much easier at the initial stage to go to the practice of laying down.

With puppies, the easiest way to practice laying is by using food motivation, that is, a treat. It is best to start training your puppy in a calm environment and in the absence of strong distracting stimuli.

How to teach the command:

You will need a treat.

Prepare a treat in your hand or a special bag. Call your dog and wait for it to sit in front of you or near your leg (depending on how you have taught it). Give the command "Down" with a gesture and voice. At the same time, a treat is in the gesture hand. Make the gesture so that the dog has time to smell the treat out. Wait up to 3 seconds. If the dog lies down, immediately give it a treat and praise it with your voice. Do not let your dog get up right away. If this happens, lay the dog mechanically. Wait 3-5 seconds, praise the dog and give a release command, for example, "Go outside". Then repeat the exercise. If after giving the command and after waiting for 3 seconds, the dog does not lie down, firmly press it on the back, thereby laying the puppy down. In this case, we praise the dog with treat after 3-5 seconds in the lying position of the dog.

Stand

Usually, training the "Stand" command begins at the age of 7 months, after the puppy has learned the commands "Sit", "Down" and began to behave more reservedly.

Just like "Sit" and "Down", the command "Stand" is worked out in a contrasting method, that is, it is equally important to use both compulsion and encouragement. Compulsion is pushing the dog under the belly, while encouragement is praise and treats.

They say that it is necessary to start acquainting the dog with the "Stand" command during examination and combing, however it is better not to do this.

How to teach:

The dog sits, we show a piece of food, pull it forward a little, the dog takes a step forward, with the other hand we hold it just under the belly. Just do not touch, but at a short distance, hold it, caress it, say that it is clever and at this moment, say "Stand" and give a piece of food.

It is very important the dog not to take many steps

forward. It has to take one step and stand up. There is a second option, when the dog is sitting, we bring food under the chest, the dog rides for a long time on the bottom. At some point, it raises its back and stands on four paws and we give the food. In this case, the dog will not step forward. It will be quickly and understandable for it that at the command "Stand" it needs to raise its back, stand on its hind legs.

The second option is when we teach the "Stand" command from the "Down" command. The dog is lying. We bring our hand palm down. We have food under our palm and thumb. The dog feels it, eats it out. We take it and turn our palm up. Together with the palm, the dog's nose will follow our hand, and it will stand up. As soon as it gets up, we give it a piece of food and at this moment we say "Stand" and praise it.

By the time the dog begins to react to the treat and gets up when it appears, it is necessary to abandon its use gradually, otherwise the dog simply will not learn to perform the command without the desired goal. Try to start to control your pet by making suggestive empty hand gestures, but be sure to reward your dog with a treat or play when it stands up.

The dog will not probably react in any way to your empty hand, in this case you should repeat the gesture; if there is still no reaction, pull or twitch the pet with the leash. When, as a result of these actions, it gets up, give it the target (delicacy). Gradually, the dog will become more and more responsive to your gestures without using the target. It means it is time to turn its attention to the voice command. To do this, make the auxiliary gesture less and less pronounced and use the leash, pulling or twitching the pet if it does not obey.

At the next stage of training, it is necessary to make a positive reinforcement of the command implementation not immediately, but with different time intervals. If the dog has done everything that it had to do, and you do not give it the desired toy or treat, then use affection: pet the dog, clap and say pleasant words in a soft voice and with a calm intonation.

Heel

Teaching a dog to walk alongside on a leash is the task of every dog breeder. The comfort of a walk together, the calmness of the dog and its owner, and the safety of the people around depend on this skill. The command "Heel" and its unquestioning accomplishment is a sign of a well-mannered and obedient dog.

Learning to walk "Heel" goes after mastering the command "Sit". All dogs, even the most stubborn ones, are able to learn the basics of correct behavior. The difference in training methods depends on the temperament of the dog, its size, age and ability.

It is easier to teach a puppy to command. You will need: a treat, a treat bag, a toy, and the help of a friend or family member to do this.

Instead of helping a friend, you can practice this exercise outside your home and grounds. Invisibly to the dog, prepare a treat in your hand behind your back. Give the command "Heel" and start a chaotic movement with turns. Pass by people and dogs if you are outside, or ask your friends to come close by if you are at home. You can also use throwing a toy as a complication. Ask friends to do it or while moving, throw it yourself. Praise your dog with a treat after each provocation if it hasn't responded to it. If the dog is distracted, cheerfully call out the nickname and the command "Heel" again. Additionally, you can use a clap on your leg.

If you are teaching an adult dog, then before practicing the command "Heel" you should draw the dog's attention:

- Stand beside and sit the dog on the left side of you.
- Call him by its nickname.
- When the dog looks at you - slap on the left hip and say "Heel".
- If the dog does not understand what to do - show it the correct position, repeat the command and clap on the hip. Repeat the steps until it masters the skill.

Teach the dog to walk next to the leg

You need to teach a puppy the command "Heel" when it is 3-4 months. Training should take 10-15 minutes with breaks. Then you can gradually increase the time to half an hour. The classes with a pet begin after a walk and play, and not immediately after leaving the house.

The skill is practiced at a different pace and with a

change in the direction of movement. The walking speed of the dog adjusts to the person. After mastering the basic course of training in a deserted place, exercises are carried out in the presence of animals and people. Important thing! Watch the dog's mood. A tired dog will not learn the lesson well.

The trained dog walks by the left side of the owner almost close to his leg. The leash is not strained. The head is raised at the level of a person's knees. When the owner stops, the dog sits down. The pet's position changes on command. If the person turns around the axis, the dog changes position and sits down again by the left leg.

At first, the dog usually falls behind the owner, runs ahead or runs to the side. In these cases, in a calm commanding intonation you give the command "Heel!" and at the same time make a jerk with a leash: forward, if the dog falls behind; backward if the dog runs ahead; to yourself if the dog moves to the side. Once the dog is in the correct position at the owner's foot, it is encouraged and you can go on moving. While practicing this technique, the owner has to ensure that the leash is always loosened, thereby giving the dog the opportunity to make mistakes (move away from the owner's leg).

After the dog has mastered the command, it is necessary to complicate the task. The owner, while moving with the dog, changes the pace, makes stops, turns in place and in motion. Changing the pace of movement, one should firstly give the command "Heel!" and only then make a jerk with a leash: forward, if the pace of movement is accelerating, and back, if the pace is slowing down. While turning in place and in motion, one also firstly gives the command "Heel!" and then make a jerk with a leash: when turning to the right - forward, when turning to the left - backwards (as if pulling the dog down). Turns in a circle with the dog are performed over the right shoulder, while the leash is jerked forward.

When is the command "Heel" given?

Before the start of the movement and before each stop. That is, say "Heel" and start moving immediately. To stop, say "Heel, sit" and stop. Make sure the dog is sitting near the left leg, not at a distance.

Before you turn to either side. If you want to turn to the right - say "Heel" and turn. If you want to turn left, say "Heel" and turn right there. If you need to go back - say "Heel" and turn back.

Before changing the pace of movement. When moving at a normal pace, say "Heel" and slow down a little. If you want to speed up - also say "Heel" and increase the pace of movement.

The "Stop" command and the "Don't do that" command

A trained dog must stop any action that is undesirable for the handler at his "Stop" command. When the command "Stop" is called out - the dog must immediately stop acting. Ideally, the Stop" command is the most irritable for the dog.

You will need a treat and 2-3 toys.

Take one toy in your hand and invite the puppy to play, freeze after 30-60 seconds, call out a nickname, pause for 1-2 seconds and give the command "Stop". The intonation should be negative, and the command itself should be sharp and on the exhalation. Don't yell at the dog. Low-toned intonation is sufficient. As soon as the puppy lets go of the toy, caress it down and give the treat. If the puppy does not let go of the toy, abruptly, but not strongly push it with your fingers into the chest or shoulder blades. When the puppy is distracted and lets go of the toy, immediately praise it with a treat and pet it. Follow this tactic for practicing the "Stop" command with other toys.

"Stop" in the distance

You will need a treat and 2-3 toys to practice this skill.

When your puppy begins to accomplish the "Stop" command perfectly near the owner, it is ready to complicate the command, namely, to accomplish it from a distance. Place some toys around the room and let the puppy in. When it is interested in one of the toys, let it play with it for 30-60 seconds. Then call out a nickname, hold for 1-2 seconds and give the command "Stop". Let me remind you that this very command is given with a negative intonation, abruptly and on exhalation. As soon as the puppy is distracted, immediately praise it emotionally with your voice. If a puppy comes up to you, praise it with a treat. Then take the same toy that the "Stop" command was directed at and play with the puppy. Then give the toy to the puppy and wait for it to choose another toy. If it does not choose a new "victim", repeat the same steps with the same toy. You can already use this command in everyday life, thereby practicing it. For example, if the puppy took something in its mouth that is not permitted to be taken or tried to steal your things from the sofa.

Command "Stop" for food

Now we will complicate the task and learn how to wean a dog from taking treats from strangers.
You will need a collar or breeching, a short leash, a regular treat and a large treat.
To begin with, put a treat in our open palm (the treat should be of such a size that the dog cannot

swallow it at once). Without giving any signals, we put our palm in front of the dog's muzzle. When dog tries to eat it, close your palm and give the command "stop", then open your palm again. We repeat until the dog begins to endure. We pause for 3-5 seconds and praise the dog with our voice and give a treat prepared in advance in a pocket. Do not give the treat from the palm of your hand. When the dog has learned to pause with a treat in the palm of your hand in front of its muzzle, you can proceed to the next step. Ask an acquaintance or a friend (who doesn't live with you) to suggest a treat. If the dog reaches for him, give the command "Stop". Praise your dog with a treat from your hand if it obeyed the command. Do not give a treat from the palm of a "stranger". If the dog does not obey the command "stop", give a slight jerk to the leash. Repeat the exercise again. Try to execute a command with different people.

Weaning to pick up from the floor.

Let us further complicate the task, we wean the dog to pick up food and garbage from the floor of the house.
You will need a collar or breeching, a regular treat and a large treat.
Practice the exercise at home. Without turning to

the dog, drop a large treat, as if by accident. The treat should be of such a size that the dog cannot swallow it at once. Observe the pet's reaction in order the dog does not notice you. When the dog tries to pick up a treat, give the command "Stop". It should be pronounced sharply, exhaling and with negative intonation. When your dog turns its attention to you, immediately praise it with a pre-prepared regular treat. Do not give a treat from the floor. If the dog does not obey the command "Stop", quickly approach the dog and give a slight jerk for the collar or breeching. When the dog is distracted, compliment it with the usual treat from your hand. If the dog managed to take the treat, take it out of the dog's mouth and throw it out on the floor in a pointed manner. If the dog does not make any attempt to pick it up, wait 3-5 seconds and praise the dog with a regular treat from your hand.

Repeat the exercise again.

After developing the skill, we complicate the task. We teach the dog not to pick it up from the floor.
You will need a collar or breeching, a regular treat and a large treat.
When your puppy has learned not to pick food off the floor in front of you, we will wean control and make the exercise more difficult. Drop a large treat

on the floor and leave the room. Pause for 3-5 seconds and come back. Praise your dog with a regular treat from your hand. If you come back and see that the dog is trying to eat a treat, say strictly "Stop", get the treat out of the mouth, if the dog managed to grab it and repeat the exercise again. When you see a stable result for 3-5 seconds, increase the time to 10-15 seconds.

Weaning to pick up from the ground on the street.

You will need a collar or breeching, a short leash, a regular treat and a large treat.

Learning not to pick up from the ground on the street slightly differs from the same within a house/apartment. Sniffing everything on the street is an important part of the puppy's socialization. Therefore, stick to the rule - "you can smell, but you cannot eat." For safe training, start by scattering your large treat and then walking past it with your dog on a leash. Allow your dog to sniff the treat if it wants to, but as soon as it starts licking it or trying to pick it up, immediately give one firm, but gentle jerk. As soon as the dog is distracted, praise it with your usual hand treat. Walk past the food again. Repeat the procedure. If your dog is sniffing or not picking up food, praise it with your treat from your hand. With each walk and practice of this exercise, scatter the treat in different areas so that the dog does not associate the command with one place.

Place

"Place" is on the list of basic commands that you need to teach a puppy or adult dog first. There are two variants of the "Place" command. In the first case, you force the dog to lie down on its home bed or sunbed, in the second, you point your hand at an object, give the command "Place", and the dog lies down next to it. Let us take a closer look at the features of this command.

Give the pet the command "Place" and lure it there

with a treat. When the dog is on his bed, praise it and give it a bite of food. Gradually increase the time between the dog's arrival and the reward, and then give the treat only occasionally. As a rule, dogs quickly understand the meaning of this command, and go to the place.

How to teach:

Take the dog on a long leash and make it lie down.

Place a large item next to it, such as a backpack. Note that this must be your item that is familiar to the dog. Do not use other people's belongings or your dog's belongings (muzzle, toy or bowl).

Repeat the "Down" command for the dog and step back 5 steps.

Wait 3 seconds and then command "Come ". When the dog comes up to you, praise it.

Give the command "Place", pointing to the backpack. To help the dog, start moving towards the object, but never jerk the leash. As you go, joyfully repeat: "Place, place, place."

Once in place, command "Down" and give a treat.

Repeat the exercise several times to train your dog to do the "Place" command well. Make the dog to go to the location without your help. Also gradually increase the distance and avoid using the leash. Ideally, the dog should walk to the thing left at a distance of up to 15 m, lie down there and wait for you to allow it to leave the position. The dog should leave the place only after your command, for example, "Go outside".

Free state

The free state is provided for the dog to rest and walk during training and daily life. The free state is also used as a reward for the dog.

The conditioned stimuli in the development of this skill are the command "Go outside!" and gesture - throwing the right hand up and down to a height slightly above the shoulder and in the direction of the desired movement of the dog with a simultaneous slight lean of the body and putting forward the right leg. The unconditioned stimulus is the natural tendency of the dog to be free. This skill is worked out parallelly with the development of skills for the commands "Heel!" and "Come!"

As soon as the puppy begins to behave in a disciplined manner and obey the owner, it can be taught to the command "Go outside!". A conditioned reflex to a command and a gesture is developed simultaneously. The exercise is performed in the following ways: the owner pulls a long leash to the collar and holds the dog near him, at the command "Walk!" in a kindly manner and gesture to the right sends the dog away from him. At the same time, it vigorously runs 5-10 m, you should repeat the command "Go outside!". Stretched out to the side hand (gesture) holds for 2-3 s, then lowers to the hip. The owner, having made a short run, gives the dog the opportunity to walk freely on a long leash. After 1-2 minutes, he calls it up by petting, gives treats for the dogs and repeats the exercise.

Jump

The command "Jump" ("Jump" or "Hop") means that the dog must jump over the specified object. When practicing this exercise, it is worth starting with quite low objects, the height of which does not exceed 10 cm (even for large dogs). Then the dog will not have the desire to lean on his paws. If you do not have a special barrier, then you can use your foot or a stick found during a walk to jump over.

To teach your dog the "Jump" command, place one foot against a wall or tree and encourage the dog to jump by attracting it over the leg with a treat or toy. Reward your dog immediately after jumping. Over time, you can increase the height of the barrier. However, do this gradually and only when your dog has repeatedly proven that it can jump the current height. Say the command "Jump" exactly at the moment when you see that the dog wants to make a jump.

When developing this skill, the following main mistakes are possible:

Premature increase in the size of obstacles without taking into account the physical capabilities of the dog and its preparedness;

Conducting classes soon after feeding;

Delay of the owner with the transition to the other side of the obstacle in the initial period;

Overworking the dog with excessively frequent and numerous jumps;

The requirement for the dog to overcome an obstacle without a run.

Teeth

"Teeth" command: this command shows the bite of the dog, and also checks if there is any extraneous object in its teeth.

Place the dog with the command "Heel".

Give the command "Teeth". Using your fingers, part your pet's upper and lower lips. Praise with your voice. After afixing the exercise, complicate it: after examining the bite, carefully open the dog's jaw and examine it. With the right skill, your dog should feel comfortable while examining its bite and mouth. Do not forget to examine your dog's mouth after a walk. Do the exercise in the same order: sit the pet on the command "Heel", command " Teeth", examine the mouth, release the dog into a free state with the command "Go outside".

Swimming

Almost all dogs can swim, the question is not how to teach a dog to swim, but how to make it love swimming. But there are exceptions: some dogs do not like swimming, because this process is difficult for them due to their structure or physiology.

Swimming is an instinctive action, and once in the water, any dog tries to swim. But you need to know that short-legged dogs, dogs with a shortened muzzle, too heavy chest and a light back part, either cannot swim, or can stay on the water for a very short time.

These breeds include Scotch Terriers, Pembroke Welsh Corgi, Bulldogs, Bassets, Dachshunds, Pugs. Greyhounds and small breeds with ample wool swim poorly - Pekingese, Shih Tzu, Lhasa Apso. There are special vests for dogs, who cannot swim in the pet industry.

It is necessary to accustom a dog to water even in puppyhood. But not earlier than they are 3 months - only after all vaccinations have been made and when there is a seasonal opportunity to get into the reservoir. The owner's job is to make the dog enjoy bathing.

If the dog swam, it does not mean that it enjoys the process. It also does not mean that it can swim for a long time. Also, if you have a breed "waterfowl" by vocation - Labrador, Golden Retriever, Spaniel, then it still does not mean that the dog from birth loves water. Like humans, dog preferences are very individual and often do not depend on belonging to a particular breed.

The first exercises in the water should not scare the dog.

1. Be patient when starting your classes. Getting your dog acquainted with water is a long process that should not be speeded up. Moreover, you should not rush if there is a bad experience, after which the dog has a fear of water.

2. Do not start classes immediately in the water. First, the dog is introduced to the reservoir in which it is planned to conduct lessons.

Unobtrusive walks are what you need. It is important that the animal gets used to the place.

3. In the second stage of training, the owner enters the water and invites the dog to join. This is where the problems most often begin: not all animals are ready to wet their paws. In this case, you can use your favorite rubber toys, kindly call your pet.

4. You can invite for a walk a familiar dog who loves to swim. Joint games will help to overcome fear: the pet will not even notice how it got into the water.

5. The first time you need to hold the dog, help it stay in the water. Even if it is ready to swim on its own.

6. It is important to keep track of how far the dog swims and how long it is in the water. Do not let your pet swim for a long time, especially at first. An animal cannot always know its own strength.

7. Don't forget about positive reinforcement. Praise your pet every time it decides to go into the water or is simply interested in it, standing on the shore.

Important!

- Only healthy vaccinated puppies over 3 months can be taught to water.
- Do not let your pet swim with a collar or leash. This is unsafe: the pet can catch on to something, especially if the reservoir is wild, and get injured.
- Do not yell at the dog, do not use physical force or force it into the water.
- It is difficult for humans to evaluate the degree of dog fatigue. But, if the pet breaths heavily, does not keep well in the water, place it in shallow water or even get out of the water.
- Swimming lessons, especially at the initial stage, should not take more than 5-10 minutes a day.

Shipping

It is very important to train your dog to the car so that you can comfortably go on a short trip (to the park) or take the dog with you for a weekend in another city.

The main advice - start accustoming your puppy to the car from a very young age, as soon as it appears in your house! A puppy is much easier to train to travel than an adult dog.

The main rule when training your dog to the car is not to rush! First, let your dog smell the car, get used to its form and smell. Never force your dog into the car. By such actions, you can discourage it from entering the car for a long time and teach it to be afraid of cars.

Let the doors to the salon be open. Give your dog the opportunity to become interested in the interior of the car. Place its favorite toys and treats on the back seat and on the floor. Give it slices of food each time it approaches the car.

Put it in the car. Let its toys and treats lie there. Don't keep it there for a long time and by force. Let it go out when it wants to.

Now you can try starting the engine. In this case, it is better that someone sits with a dog in the back seat. If the dog starts to get nervous, do not pet it, otherwise you will only reinforce its fear. Behave as if nothing is happening, be absolutely calm. Turn off the engine, release the dog. Release your dog when it is calm and does not rush out.

Feed your dog in the car with the doors closed.

Now you can make a short trip of 5-10 minutes. There should be someone with the dog in the back seat. But don't comfort it. Be calm yourself - it will be transmitted on to the dog.

Important! Do not feed your dog before driving to avoid vomiting.

Gradually increase the distance and duration of your trips.

Important! Your puppy can get seasick in the car, so

it is worth covering the salon of your car with something on the first trips.

When teaching, follow the rule of gradualism and sequence. Don't take long trips right away.

The first trips should in no way be associated with something unpleasant (a visit to the veterinarian, for example). When studying, only pleasant associations should be related with a trip - a walk to a forest, a park, to the friends.

In order your pet does not get bored on the trip - take its toys with you.

It is also important to remove fragrances from the car.

To prevent the dog from getting seasick on the road, train it to the car with daily trips for 15 minutes.

You should:

1. Teach the dog to enter and leave the car on command.
2. It is necessary to teach the dog to remain alone in the car, just as you teach it to stay alone at home, gradually increasing the time of your absence. But you cannot leave the dog in the car for a long time.
3. Be sure to train your dog to a certain place in the car so that it does not disturb you while

you are driving and does not climb on your hands or caress and lick the driver.

4. Train your dog to ride in the back seat instead of on the floor.

5. If you want to carry your dog in the front seat - transport it on the floor in the passenger seat or in special containers.

6. When transporting your pet, use special accessories.

If you are planning to transport your dog by plane or train, then you need:

1. Transport cage

It is necessary to accustom the dog to it in advance. If the animal suddenly finds itself in an enclosed space, this can provoke panic and a nervous breakdown.

Important:

Transporting animals on an aircraft is permitted by most airlines' regulations, but transportation requirements may vary. Therefore, try to contact the airline you are flying with as soon as possible in order to find out its conditions and to book a seat in time.

The dog on the plane must be in a container designed for this.

To transport an animal, the passenger is obliged to provide a container, a cage of sufficient size with air access. Without a cage/container - transportation is strictly prohibited. The bottom of the container (cage) must be waterproof and covered with an absorbent material. The animal should be able to stand up "full height" and turn around its axis. The lock must be secure.

2. Water

Fresh cool water should be in the dog's bowl at all times. The trip is no exception. Stock up on enough drinking water and make stops (especially if the journey is long) so that the dog can stretch its legs and drink. It is usually recommended to do this at least every three to five hours.

3. First aid kit

If your dog suffers from any chronic illness, make sure that all the necessary medications are on hand.

4. Veterinary passport

Wherever you go, the dog's veterinary passport must be with you. On long journeys by train or plane, your pet will simply not be taken on board without it.

How to prepare your dog for the ride:

- Before traveling with the dog, take a good walk. Increase the time of the habitual exercise so that the dog can do all the necessary activities;
- Give the dog a drink of water;
- Do not feed the dog just before the trip - it can get seasick;
- If the trip is going to be a long one, the dog should be given food at least an hour before the planned departure;
- Do not create additional stress factors, which include, for example, too loud music or careless driving.

Printed in Great Britain
by Amazon